Reflections

Katherine Lee Lee

BookLeaf
Publishing

Presentation by *BookLeaf Publishing*

Web: www.bookleafpub.com

E-mail: info@bookleafpub.com

ISBN: 9789357615976

First edition 2022

This collection of special poems are dedicated to my loving family. May my memories live forever in your hearts

Mom

ACKNOWLEDGEMENT

Many thanks to my dear family and friends who encouraged me from the very beginning. Also, a special thank you to a very dear friend, Kelly, for encouraging me to pursue this lifelong dream with a 21 day writing challenge.

Moments

I thank the Lord for beautiful
moments,
Spread throughout my years.
They bring me joy and comfort,
They wash away my fears.

Twinkling stars, moonlit nights ,
Sunsets that beam with Grace.
Endless snowflake patterns,
Hydrangeas that resemble lace.

Knowing that you are here for me,
Is more than I deserve.
My love for you is endless,
Teach me how to serve.

But most of all you've Blessed,
The greatest gift to me.
Three tiny souls to nurture, love and trust,
Then proudly set them free.

Together As One

I will hold your hand when you are lonely,
I will touch your heart when you fear.
My love for you is stronger than,
The colors of a rainbow appear.

I am there when you trip in the darkness.
I am there when you fall out of line.
I am there when never a moment goes right,
I am there in the trust of time.

I am there when your faith is shallow,
And your tomorrow's seem light years away.
I will always be there to help you,
My son, you shall not stray.

If there ever comes a time in your life,
When the colors just seem to fade away.
Look up to the heavens and reach for the stars,
And together as one, we will pray.

God's Gift

We all enter this world,
With a white canvas of snow.
While we inherit traits from our past,
Our canvas continues to grow.

Your paint brush is held by you,
The artist of your soul.
Create a life to be proud of,
Honest, faithful and whole.

Fill your canvas with lots of color,
Discrimination shall not exist.
Add a splash of caring and tenderness,
For the poor, the homeless and sick.

Be generous with your earnings,
It's more than you possibly need.
The feeling that molds your heart,
Is like a harvest from only one seed.

When you think you have completed your
artwork,
Know that it will change along the way.
Make the most of God's gift-Life,
Feel proud at the end of the day.

P.S. Hang your picture on your heart for all to
see!

Be Thankful

The sun rises, the sun sets,
Another moon is full.
The flowers bloom on endless love,
For years of life to fulfill.

The time from learning to love each other,
To a time caring for child.
We continue to grow, as life told us so…
"Be thankful & graciously smile."

The challenges of life are so demanding,
But the pleasures are ever endured.
The moments that happened yesterday,
Are the blessings that keep us assured.

Thank you dear Lord for all:
My love, my life, my faith.
Without a drop of your blessings,
My heart would feel unsafe.

So Blessed

Lace curtains danced as the morning sun rose.
A gentle breeze whispered-"So Blessed."
A moment frozen in time,
The heart of my family nest.

The rocker from Papa gently swayed,
As the wooden floor softly creaked.
Baby laid snuggled in love,
In my arms fast asleep.

I gaze at the beauty, only God can create.
An innocent child, so perfect, so great.
Blessings continued,
As God deemed so-
    Three babies to love…
    Three babies to glow…

Memories

It's fun to be a kid again,
To play morning till night.
To wake with stickers in our hair,
And sleep while holding Teddy tight.

Cheerios for breakfast,
Peanut butter and bananas at noon.
A snack in the old sandbox,
Daddy is coming home soon.

Around the table we hold hands and say,
"Jesus loves me", We bow and pray.

Bath time is awesome, Imagination gone wild.
I am a pirate, a dolphin, a child.

Being a parent takes me back in time,
When I was little, when I was nine.

Endless Love

The rise of the sun is all I needed,
To start a beautiful day.
But that all changed when I saw your smile,
A Blessed sunshine ray.

Being a mom is very special,
Being first in line for all.
But Mimi is an endless love,
That is available in a heartbeat, a teardrop, a
call.

Whether we bake, clean, Garden or dance,
A lesson you learn from a book.
Mimi always includes Jesus' love,
And the sacrifice for us He took.

A Poppi is a special man,
Whose shoes are hard to fill.
Despite his talent of non-judgemental love,
His tools include heart, soul and will.

On the floor is where he is,
Playing face to face.
With gentle eyes and a warming touch,
Poppi handles his babies with grace.

As our generations of family continue to grow,
Our hearts will never cease.
To have the love sufficient for all,
To dwell in God's presence and peace.

Another Blessed New Day

I close my eyes and pray in peace,
And speak to the Lord above.
The end of the day is reserved for us,
A slot labeled "True Love".

I thank with open heart,
Family and friends you gave.
I thank you for the precious times,
That my soul will always crave.

Thank you for the endless love,
That only you can provide.
You reassure that all is well,
You dry the tears I've cried.

I thank you for the memories,
I refuse to ever let go.
I so appreciate my parents,
How I miss them so.

The sacrifices that were made for me,
The love I thought was nill.
Now comes alive from up above,
As you guide me & strengthen my will.

Good night, dear Lord in the heavens above,

Thank you for hearing me pray.
I am ready to sleep,
Covered with assurance and love,
I am now prepared for "Another New Day".

Listen

The power and strength from above,
Is better than food and drink.
It nourishes our hearts and souls.

If only the world would listen…

Power and strength from above,
Consoles the pain of the hurting.
It heals the loss and comforts the heart.

If only the world would listen…

The power and strength from above,
Guides one to trust and respect.
We are all brothers from the same Divine.

If only the world would listen…

The Lord created us with love and compassion,
Respect, honor and joy.
Let us do the same,
One emotion at a time.

I think the world is listening…

For All To See

Upon the roof so high in the sky,
Symbol of love to remind us why.

Along the roadside up high on a hill,
The love of Jesus to remind us still.

Young or old, black or white,
It is there for all-
What a beautiful site.

The steeple of a church will always be,
A true reminder of why Jesus died for me.

"Come in, sit down and pray with thee,
I am your Savior;
Your Glory Be".

Gifts From Above

The world is full of gifts,
That only you can wrap.
Every day is full of presents,
You place them in our laps.

Today a pretty flower,
Appeared so bright and blue.
It smelled so warm and tender,
It reminded me of you.

Next I found a raindrop,
So perfect, round and wet.
I felt like I was melting,
In the joy when we first met.

As the day flew by the hour,
The presents continued to appear.
I saw a pretty rainbow,
Smiling ear to ear.

You are my blessed Savior,
You are my pride and love.
Thank you Lord for all the gifts,
My gifts from up above.

Deep In My Heart

Memories of my childhood,
Will never fade away.
They are imbedded in my heart in gold,
Shining brilliant throughout my days.

The smell of hay in Grandpa's barn,
The potato roasting long.
The kitchen table that fed us all,
The swing that sang my song.

The endless cookies to decorate,
The pony that refused to budge.
The lime green paint that lit my room,
My sisters to hold a grudge.

The pump of red that cleaned our feet,
The clothesline mom kept full.
The frozen pond to slide our skates,
The toboggan to loaded to pull.

The fondest memory that warms my heart,
Is the love that decorated the walls.
Words of gentle kindness,
Still echo through the halls.

Tranquility

I am surrounded by peace,
Tranquility sheaths my day.
No bitterness or jealousy,
Can stand in the way.

Joy fills my hands with tenderness,
And misty drops of dew.
The purest scent of fragrance,
Is greatly welcomed too.

The sheer abundance amazes me,
How beauty fills my all.
The tender petals so loving,
Captures the season of fall.

Hydrangeas are a gift from God,
That blesses my soul with love.
If this one plant can change my life,
They must fill the heavens above.

The Lesson

The eyes of a child see so much more,
Then the rich man's pocket can hold.
The tender love in their innocent eyes,
Forgives all untold.

What a wonderful world this place would be,
If only we were four.
We would be holding hands and singing songs,
Instead of closing doors.

To each we need a lesson,
On how to love and proclaim.
No matter the rainbow color,
God loves us all the same.

Behind Closed Doors

A fear has stricken the world afar,
A fear of unknown and despair.
It has shaken souls and broken hearts,
A distruction beyond repair.

A time of loss of so many lives,
The sick dying alone.
Families unable to share their grief,
The feel of human contact unknown.

The touch of a hand once comforting and warm,
Is now replaced by a phone.
The lies be hidden, the truth be untold,
Loved one's passing behind closed doors-alone.

Dear sweet Jesus, please help us now,
Our love will never cease.
We trust that we will be safe in your arms,
Please guide us with your gracious peace.

Grace & Trust

My love for you is tender,
My love for you is true.
The thought of everlasting life,
Is my dream when I pray to you.

I know I am not perfect,
I tend to wander and stray.
But yet your hand of gentle touch,
Bestows me on my way.

You remind me of the cross on the hill,
The gentle words of the land.
The perfect sacrifice you proclaimed that night,
As you placed your life in His hands.

Dear God, give me the strength I need,
To follow your steps in the sand.
To live a life full of Grace & Trust,
To live my life so grand.

Joy To All

The bells may be joyfully ringing,
And the children merrily singing.
The Christmas time is here,
But now I've come to realize
The reason Jesus appeared.

He came to save the world from sin,
He came from up above.
But not to bring us presents,
But to sprinkle the world with love.

He loves us through his music.
He teaches us through his song.
The messages that are sent from above,
Preach rightly about truth and love.

So listen very carefully,
As you walk through the life on end.
Our everlasting Savior,
Is really your everlasting friend.

My Heroes

A star in his eye, a stripe in his smile,
Bravery touches his soul.
A commitment to his country,
Sights and sounds to never be told.

A fear that comes with a value,
That only a soldier can hide.
The safety of others a priority in time,
He faces the thorn in his side.

The dangers await him daily,
As he stands eager, ready and vowed.
His uniform is only material,
It's his heart that makes us proud.

Over 75 years have passed,
As we celebrate the end of World War II.
Photos can never tell the stories,
The way a soldier knew.

My uncle sits in his wheelchair,
With a tear still lingering in his eye.
While a nephew took his place in line,
All for America to survive.

May God bless and keep you both safe,

May a rainbow guide you through.
Fly high and wave those American flags,
Hold true to the red, white and blue.

Spread The Gift

I am a little bundle,
All snuggled tight & warm.
As you hold me in your loving arms,
You protect me from the storm.

I am a curious toddler,
Exploring my beautiful world.
You guide me step-by-step,
As I learn to love the Lord.

I am a doubting teen,
I will always question "why".
Your answer whispers in the wind,
"Your faith and I abide".

My days are fading fast,
But my faith is ever so strong.
Thank you Lord, for all you have done,
You have never steered me wrong.

Life is but a moment,
That blinks away so fast.
Share the love that the Lord has made,
Spread the gift that will last.

Someday

Someday in heaven
We will see eye to eye.
Nothing will matter
Except you & I.

There will be no more government,
No Kool-Aid to drink.
The pandemic will be conquered,
The world will be in sync.

Hatred and prejudice,
will be a thing of the past,
We will be all Gods'
children,
In heaven at last.

All languages will form music,
All colors will blend.
Our children will embrace,
"United We Stand".

I will send up my poem,
To heavens bright light.
And pray that my "someday",
Will happen"tonight".

Friends For Life

I have a favor buddy,
Who is very special to me.
She entered my life as a birthday surprise,
Her name is Shadow Lee!

She runs and jumps and keeps me young,
With sticks, balls and toys.
I never knew her loving eyes,
Could fill my heart with joy.

The years went by, the love grew deeper,
As we both experienced some greys.
To snuggle up with the warmth of her heart,
Her devotion shined through each day.

We will always be together,
No matter where we roam.
We may not be physically joined,
Someday, again we will be home.

Another birthday surprise came,
Another for a bundle of glee.
Another bond of friendship to build,
But this time with Happy Lee!